STALIN'S CARNIVAL

BOOKS BY STEVEN HEIGHTON

FICTION

Flight Paths of the Emperor
On earth as it is
The Shadow Boxer
Afterlands
Every Lost Country
The Dead Are More Visible

POETRY

Stalin's Carnival
Foreign Ghosts
The Ecstasy of Skeptics
The Address Book
Patient Frame

ESSAYS

The Admen Move on Lhasa
Workbook: memos & dispatches on writing

CHAPBOOKS/LETTERPRESS

Paper Lanterns: 25 Postcards from Asia
The Stages of J. Gordon Whitehead

STALIN'S CARNIVAL

STEVEN HEIGHTON

The first edition was published by Quarry Press, Kingston, 1989. Permission to reprint was granted by the author.

Palimpsest Press
5 King St. Kingsville, Ontario. N9Y 1H9
www.palimpsestpress.ca

Book and cover design by Dawn Kresan. Typeset in Minion Pro and Niagara Solid, and printed offset on Rolland Zephyr Laid at Coach House Printing in Ontario, Canada.

Palimpsest Press would like to thank the Canada Council for the Arts, and the Ontario Arts Council for their support of our publishing program. We also acknowledge the assistance of the Government of Ontario through the Ontario Book Publishing Tax Credit.

Canada Council for the Arts Conseil des Arts du Canada ONTARIO ARTS COUNCIL CONSEIL DES ARTS DE L'ONTARIO Ontario Ontario Media Development Corporation

LIBRARY AND ARCHIVES CANADA
CATALOGUING IN PUBLICATION

Heighton, Steven
Stalin's carnival / Steven Heighton.

Poems. ISBN 978-1-926794-14-3

I. TITLE.
PS8565.E451S7 2013 C811'.54 C2012-908552-9

For my father

CONTENTS

Man to the Hills

INTRODUCTION

It's good news for readers that Steven Heighton's debut collection, *Stalin's Carnival*, is available again in a new edition. Any poet of Heighton's accomplishment, commitment, and range, still gaining readers now, in mid-career, through equally impressive stories, novels, and poetry, should not have to witness the premature disappearance of their early work.

To employ that sly little descriptor, 'early work,' so often flags a creeping apology or caveat, as though we'd be well-advised to read with an eye to the binder marked 'juvenilia.' This simply is not the case here. Heighton's enduring and consistent themes, and the tropes he employs to investigate them, are all here in force. Erotic and familial love, the body's kinetic energies, a mature awareness of time's designs on that body, history manifest in the present, violence, death, and our stubborn urge to sing in its shadow. Heighton seemed to be zeroing in on the eternal themes of lyric verse right out of the gate, yet his real sophistication shows its mark in how very many of these poems insist on embedding or naturalizing the heart's concerns in a pulsing, tactile, dynamic context and frame. The poems are a picture of the world first—and within that recognizable theatre we watch the poem wrestle its devils to no clean decision.

'Wrestle' works here, but so would any number of terms lifted from athletics, dance, labour, or music. I read *Stalin's Carnival* as a very young man, while bashing around in 20th century poetry trying to erect a scale model in my head of what a poem could look like now. Hearing the vibrancy and veering turns and wind-sprint syntax in these poems lit me up long before I'd begun to think through their thematic worries. Is it OK to be first drawn to the action? Exactly how Heighton's poems plummeted down the page excited me then and I wanted to learn from them.

This collection has ambition, crisis, honesty, music, heart-break, and beauty all placing the human voice under a severe strain, and the voice is up to it.

—Ken Babstock, Toronto, January 2013

AUTHOR'S NOTE

To reread and revise a book you wrote half a lifetime ago is a daunting prospect. Many would say it's best not to do it at all. But if *Stalin's Carnival* is to come back into print—it's been unavailable since 1994, five years after it was published—I owe it to prospective readers to comb through it for obvious howlers and, I feel, cull the weakest poems.

I have a precedent for this process. In 2000, I went back into my first two fiction books, the story collections *Flight Paths of the Emperor* and *On earth as it is*, to prepare new editions. The Porcupine's Quill had first published the books in 1992 and '95 respectively. Vintage Canada was to reissue them in 2001. As I went over the originals, I worked out a rule: I could make small fixes, such as altering words that seemed plainly wrong, or hacking out dead adverbs and fanciful adjectives (one change I recall: substituting the correct "trowel" for the wordy, imprecise, and oddly brainless "small hand shovel"). At the same time, I disqualified myself from making changes that violated the character or spirit of a story. After all, I'd been a different man when I wrote it. I figured that if I superimposed the sensibility of a forty-year-old on a story written by someone in his late twenties, I'd create an awkward or monstrous hybrid—and possibly mute a valuable vitality. Youth should have its say, and it only gets one chance. If I found the spirit of a story too immature, I would simply have to cut it. (In one case, I did.)

In 2006, I tested this precedent while working with Dawn Kresan of Palimpsest Press to create a chapbook—beautifully illustrated with photos by Mary Huggard—out of my second poetry collection, *Foreign Ghosts* (Oberon, 1990). It had been out of print for years and during that time I'd come to feel that, through no fault of the original publisher, the book contained a lot more pages than poems. So in preparing what was to become *Paper Lanterns: 25 Postcards From Asia*, my main task was to winnow the text down to twenty-five pieces (poems or journal entries), then tweak them as necessary, in keeping with the principle that I could revise only phrasing, never the impulse or spirit of the work.

In readying this re-issue of *Stalin's Carnival* I've followed that same principle—altering or cutting wrong or lazy words and lines, and sometimes, for acoustical or semantic reasons, nudging punctuation and line-breaks, while cutting outright four poems that struck me as too flawed to remain even in a first book. In essence, though, this is still very much that book.

I'm grateful to Robert Hilderley of Quarry Press for encouraging me to complete the original collection. I'm also grateful to Dawn Kresan for bringing out this new edition. Finally, my thanks to the House of Anansi for generously granting reprint permission for a few poems that, while they debuted in *Stalin's Carnival*, later appeared in collections I've published with Anansi.

—SH, Kingston, November 2012

ENERGY IS ETERNAL DELIGHT

ENDURANCE

1

At the crack she pounced
hours over the grip of pool, she split
the skin and sheered like a seawind back

to breast the surface, ripple with fluid
motion toward a standing wall. She coiled,
sprang, and her back broke

water, fin-slick, arched again and drove.
Someday the water's skin will not give,
its flesh will stiffen around her, gathering

strands of her hair and strength, and spirit them
down like a moon through the tidal pools.
Her crawl will slacken but discover in rest

the power of sea-beds, mussels, coral
that forge in the rhythms of sleep a pearl
of flesh. See her flail with brief endurance—

when the race ends, there is still this.

2

Entering the delta her stroke is eased
by spring currents, she is breathing in first
smells of salt and faint rumours
of seagrape, kelp and
coldwater coral.
She has come down to this
lowland where the waters break
against her swimming skin and all its reaches, arms,
the gleaming mouths she has opened
with cupped fingers.
The river is always giving up its daughters,
sons, where the waters run to green
districts the living and half-living only half-conceive;
when at first crack she pounced
between white margins of a pool, she vanished
through the surface into tarns
where waters shone and loafed, into rills
and diving rapids, the engorged
rivers of the low country. Then great lakes
descending to the delta. Into spring currents.
With the larger fish:
sturgeon, marlin, white whale
gliding, she is generations in the long canal
travelling each season of her blood, she brooks
the tides in the estuary, breakers out from the coast until
she is only us, receding, a floating pulse,
the foamed bloodroar
required by the undertow.

SAILING, GULF ISLANDS

Let me remember

my father. How he
swooped like a diving gull under the swung
boom and we ran
steady, before the winds in early evening
failed.
Sail's flap
and sweet strain in a fathering gust,
how I gripped whiteknuckled and leaned
years back
till scud and the speed-
warm sea slapped
in my hair, my father

there with the rudder kept the stone-
fragrant shores to port, to bright star-

board a blue vaulting of shoalcold spaces
banked with windwall and towering cloud—

I remember now
like a conscious poet
that fugitive harmony,
child's sphere,
half my brain asleep, the other teeming, almost
curled in the cool sail's belly
till the wind died.

Lies,
I dredge them up again, again and run
aground on the steaming seacoasts I recall,

or do I invent
those graveyards of the dreamed Pacific—

Face rimed with salt I am still
that child leaning back,
a craft standing at anchor
in the sounds and green havens of fiction.

ICARUS

The idea of motion he describes:

in sunlight, pending,
a sinuous figure fathers the air-
graced fall from abstraction, free

of the diving board's stutter; that first vain
clutching at sun reversed
by gravity, the pistilled flower pulled down. Bending

back into first geometry
(algebra of garden or woodpool, square-
root of the orchid) he descends like rain

to his failure, equating skin with the undispersed
water, dying and saving us.
And because every feat is a fall into broken

silence, like any creator
for him to win is to disappear, as a poet,
moving, becomes the surface of a page,

as the dreams of an Icarus persist under sea.
And this is the layering. As he breaks with pen-
straight arms the pool

blooms dewcold round him, stirred
drops dissolve into calm, and silence
swallows the feet disappearing into green

water. But already a form, a word
has passed into the surface.
Impossible to say how many were watching.

HIGH JUMP

Four strides the legs compass, close,
burst gravity's shell and vault

as sunrise at the pole bends
back, sickles the sun-

sleek arc of dolphin, diver, gull,
his skull at noon and hovering. There

the body contends with higher things—
sharp light, thinning air; the eclipse

and setting of records; a fixed
orbit he believes he frames. At his height

he wavers, reels like a lover and prays
his lunging survives him

in a perfect act; feels time
tug at his second hand

as the earth draws breath, pole
and body into ground. Hear it:

a hissing of wind in the high
arena, and his spikes

rattle, raised like knuckles at the sky.

SKATERS

Like Brueghel's children on the brilliant ice-
tableau I can see them, tracing
circuits in vaulting air, the skaters
skimming, reeling in random
loops that flower and scrawl the whole
dissolving surface. But
who will paint them (sing them,
say them) in this, their own winter—
a season not very like the brief
Belgian winter in triptychs you unfold
and fasten at will. The skaters,
with no fences to skirt or history
to frame them, leave on the canvas-
white lake ice
their own artifice
to thaw in time and fracture
like a fifteenth-century icon.

And though their muscles remember
for a time
every arc and stride, each line inscribed
against impartial weather, I would see them
from the sky's blank dome, a watcher
in the scaffolding, marking
their progress, and maybe

saving
this northern lake
flecked with little characters
like the plains of Flanders,
millpools, gardens,
frozen by the painter's hand.

And like the painter I would add
hours off in the middle distance
a range of mountains
that never really were:
high polders against the sea,
steepled over the little kirks
and barren woodlots, the hunters
coming home through snow
and the skaters . . .

Mountains:
the only forms
the artist could devise
to dwarf those gliding
flawless folk
who paint the ice
like rivals—

ARCHER

The clock insists seconds
but for the watcher
for the archer himself
the poise before firing
is an epoch
no timekeeper marks
and the moment
before release is primed,
like the belly of a stringed instrument
before one strums,
with music, pent;
or like muscle, tensed;
like staves kept breathless
as a blank page
or target.

And the other silence:
inaudible harmony
of arms and string
vibrating.
No one is left to score it.

ROWERS

The clasping, the pulling taut
with arms gone leaden, is reflex, rote.
The rhythm is learned, grown automatic.
What is hard is the blind
backward gliding, unseeable speed
and another's eyes for yours.

You are part of the craft you row.
With your breathing stern, back bowed,
each stroke ticks hours in the mouth
of the harbour; and as the furrow you carve there
fades, as your breaths expire into distance,
it is hard, the blind, backward
gliding, unseeable speed
and the peering eyes.

                                        A poet
drives his craft, her craft
with no more promise than this
blindness, this signature that will always settle
into an unstirred plane. There's that moment you burst
cold water with your blade
and the race rewards you;
there's that moment arms waver and the surface won't part
with secrets no one wanted to hear
at any rate:

when the stroke is done
and you sag over oar-locks,
there's still a form in the scull,
a voice that coaxes
look back:
see the empty sound

you're leaving behind you

and no one to sing it if you find the quay

SOLO

(A slight form   black
on a smooth snowbridge
crossing in the clear
distance
                where ice is honed   blade-
blue   the sun
staggering

eyes are daggered with edged light)

                                                                  Balanced
on the iceface
imagine a mind and eyes
challenging this equilibrium

there are no eyes in the iceface

and as you clamber with uneasy skill
the partner roped above you
is intent on her own calculations . . .

Climbing   like a death
is done alone   a solo into mountains
there are no audience expectations
and if there are watchers
they are too far off to see things as you do

                                 One time in the Maligne Range you remember
feet kicking rungs into ice
and finding a spot sunsoftened
                                                        —boot slipped
                                                                          for a breath-

span you taloned the ice
with ice-axe   fingernails   every cell of you gripping

in your eyes the blurred circuit of a valley entire
as you glanced back
over ranks of stunted trees
and the empty amphitheatre
echoing

Afterward
intimate embrace of cold
faults in the ice   the fear of hours
of vacant space
and layered atmospheres conspiring

High above you a thin spine of cirrus
severed itself against the peak

                                        and after the plummeting first fear
in the belly had passed
it was this strangeness that remained unsettling

That the world was a stage perhaps
but few had ever been watching
That death
an act of ideal intensity
could be swallowed discreetly in a blue crevasse
under a canopy of neutral cloud

That even the sharpest cry must go unnoticed
and the sum of everything you'd ever believed
or said
came to a soliloquy delivered one evening
to a row or two of empty chairs

Maligne Amphitheatre, Alberta

GRAVE BY RAPIDS

dated 1892
Rifle Chutes, Madawaska

This sound
this rushing is

a black teeming
of driven water
narrowing hard in a downstream V

and shouting: ours
the suck of keepers
loud by boulders'
foaming thrash

and there the current
with brutal ease
dug nails in keel
clenched the stern
and shot us down

saw death
the white of foam
a breath
and streams slid running
shoreless green—

ENTROPY

1

When the race ends there is still
water, lapping stone shores
to slow powder, plunge
of fish's plash and vanishing
in the distance, in an empty bay—
In a while, wind
off the water might lisp and
barrow the beach, enter a forest, clatter
boughs and bicker at the eaves and sills
of an ash-cold cabin—
On the bay a loon
dives in a plummet of white
thread spooled into darkness.
Somewhere in the forest a tree
is falling in perfect silence.

Still
there will be no silence,
not completely, not
while you can read this
page, *this*
page, speak the words aloud or
better, this: put the book down,
turn, walk from your room and head
quickly as if with reason down the fire-alley
the backstreets the sideroad into fields and further
into woodlots beginning to run
over blazing quires of leaves
on a day in October dying, you
halo yourself with breath, circuit the square fields, your limbs

naked and no need now for dust-
jackets or book-
ends, you dancer, you
hurl up your bare white heels: two moons
quicker than symbols on the page
and singing—

When the race ends there is only
the rich vacuum after song.

2

In Dresden tongues of fire fell
from screaming clouds, consuming the testaments
of ascetics, scholars, remote saints
who bled their last life in ink, gambled
on a tenuous stamina, and lost
after a handful of indifferent centuries.
                                                            In Alexandria
the scrolls must have blazed like torches and cast
a flickering light on the calm sea
for an evening, then embered
to reticent ash;
                        by the morning
histories, whole lexicons
had vanished—

                        And even runes
engraved in a stone
cliff face
by the artisans of some northern tribe

weather and peer blankly

into winds prevailing from the west

                                                            or

gazing up   discern

                                        like a dying chieftain

an epitaph

                        of thin high clouds eroding at dusk

CARNIVAL

The hall can't hold them. Crazed
With heat and flailing arms they stamp
Into the streets, stopping traffic, tap-
Dancing on the polished hoods
Of factory-new cars. Frantic
Owners invoke order, but it's no use at all—the amazed
Mounted Police retreat, their lathered horses prancing
With abandon, hoofs
Clopping the pavement like castanets.

We must act quickly. We need fire-hoses, nets
And weapons. Already lines are down and have been seen
Tangled with bare limbs in the backstreets, construction
Fences shattered, walls defaced
With long lines of spraypaint
Verse and graffiti. These dancers
Will have to be dealt with, an answer
Of some suitable form
Found, but there are factors to explore:
Scholars to consult for explanations,
Philosophers about ramifications . . . The governor however
Knows there is no time. Firm as Stalin
He calls in troops, police and black leather
Squadrons that quickly arrive
To an orchestra of sirens, soprano tires, all masters of the organized
Art of marching. Through the madness goosestepping soldiers
Crack stiff salutes and muster
In neat stanzas on the crowded square
but the crowd has not come to obey. They twist instead
to a staccato of shots, hurl themselves at the machine-
gunners till wildflowers
bloom in barrels like a fable.

The city is infected. Even secretaries are
kissed by St Vitus and dance
to the clatter of pressed keys.
                                        In the office whole stacks
of correspondence tumble
or flutter like confetti from the company
president's window, and he too is seen in Bermuda
shorts and baggy shirt
jigging to the beat
                                 They are so out of hand now, so
out of hand—the drunken musicians perform
from aerial, chimney and beerhall-
poets arrive to urge them on
and on it goes with wild imperfect rhymes
the tired reporters sent to the scene are soon drumming
sewergrates with broken pens   there are
no words now but rhythm they reel
like Ogun Shiva & Jesus together
in celebration the world hurtles
                                          springs
                                                 & at last

dionysus is spotted at the mob's edge
   spinning with ogun shiva &
                                          jesus
  even buddha breaks his trance
joins the carnival & belly
     dances with the best of them

ASHES ON THE EARTH: SELECTED WORKS OF JOSEF STALIN

Only in Russia is poetry respected; it gets people killed. Is there anywhere else where poetry is so common a motive for murder?

—Osip Mandelstam

BIOGRAPHY

In his early poems Stalin makes no effort to conceal his emotions, and he shows clearly that he was capable of genuine religious feeling and possessed a romantic attachment to the oppressed, following a centuries-old poetic tradition. Already there is evidence of a small but real poetic talent.

—Robert Payne, *The Rise and Fall of Stalin*

Before he became
arguably the most expert
mass-murderer of an era noted for its butchery
Josef Djugashvili Stalin of Soviet Georgia
was a promising poet.

A romantic by temperament
he magnified the names
of spirited forebears,
skies of the homeland
and resolute martyrs
whose banners read fervently
freedom—

In some poems one can feel
the harsh grandeur of the Caucasus,
Georgian slopes and orchards
are evoked with the power
of dedicated, sensitive men
and women, sheets in hand

who felt the music pulse in marrow
the wind that blew through pores
the tears of the world, the "light
in lovers' eyes"—

years later he strangled his wife
and slew twenty million others

1. TO THE MOON

Move on, inexhaustible one—
Never bowing your round, scarved head,
Scatter the misty clouds,
Great is the providence of the Almighty.
Gaze gently upon the busy world
That lies outspread beneath you;
Sing a hymn to the peak where Prometheus died
Still rising like a steeple through the air.
Know well that those who once fell
Like ashes on the earth, who long ago
Succumbed to the oppressors
Will rise again and soar, winged with hope,
Above the sacred mountain.
And as in bygone days
You glowed among the clouds,
Let your rays now play in splendour
Over the brilliant sky.
I shall tear like paper my silver blouse
And bare my breast to the moon
And with outstretched hands
Praise her who suckles the world with light.

for my mother, August 1895

(Freely adapted from Josef Stalin's second published poem, which appeared in the liberal-progressive Georgian literary periodical Iveria, *October 1895)*

2. ELEGY

Father, you will be for me always
The shadow of the onion spire chasing me home
Through dust at sundown up the Sobarnaya.
You will be for me always
The great drinker, great brawler whom men
Of our street defame since his departure
Without warning to a shallow grave. Father
You will be for me always
The cruel rhetorician, the bell-voiced actor
Who made a plank table his pulpit, a fist his scripture,
A wife and child his battered congregation.
                                        You will be for me always
The onion spire that hung at your thighs
When you bathed, the virile aroma
Of your breath and body,
Mortal as incense, foreign as the ikons
That made your room a forbidden chamber
Steeped in mysterious powers. Father
You will be for me always
Those black brows like a hawk's wings arching
Avid of prey, you will be for me beatings
We must have deserved
Though you would not give us a reason, father,
You will be these things though you have left, you will stay
My teacher, my shadow, you
Drunk as a cobbler, boot-nails and brandy,
Hammer at the throat, you deity, Father,
I am nailed to the future
You will be for me always.

1896 *for Vissarion* (?–1890)

3. ON READING DARWIN

From the shore I watched a cargo of chickens
Spill from a barge into the river.
Trapped in their wooden cages they floated
Momentarily in the freezing currents, then mutant
With fear, attacked one another, turned
Into fighting cocks, quarrelling,
Screeching, bleeding as their barred
Coffins filled with water.

From the riverbank I saw the bargemen
Forfeiting profit for a moment's diversion
And laughing at the disappearing birds
I thought of hungry schools
Of fish scuttling through the bars
Like the scoured ribs of drowned sailors
And white wings beating an idle descent
Through an evolving darkness.
From the riverbank I saw their feathers
Form alien words on the face of the waters;
At first I could not read them and I was afraid.

The seminary, 1896

4. EKATERINA

With her death the last shards of compassion in me
Are crushed. For too long I have squinted at the world
Through sheets of stained glass: the deep
Scarlet of sacrificial wounds, Christ's passion, the crimson
Fingers of a tyrant Father. I walk from the churchyard
For the last time. Will you walk with me? I promise
We will not look back. No moving shade
Of pane could temper death's spectrum, or alter
The cast of my recollections. All dead. I regret everything
But the future. Walk beside me for your own good.
I shall drive histories before me like a flock of lambs.

1905

(By this alchemy the glass of introspection is changed
to the steel of pure activity. The lens and scope
become the iron barrel.
An intercession of many years,
civil war, victory, railroads and hydroelectric dams,
provinces burning in the nerves of Stalin.
Another marriage. A honeymoon.)

5. 1921: AN ORDER TO THE RED ARMY NEAR ROSTOV

Call it the return of the prodigal son.
Call it anarchy, call it order. Why should I care
what you call it? Call it murder.
Yes, take this down, all of it. Call it
an order.
"Posterity expects one of two things
from its engineers: firmness coupled with regret
over savage necessity, or else
the remorseless will to urge all means
to their imperative endings. With no regret.

"People are thrilled by any stranger
unafraid of the power they fear. History
stalls without electricians. Rusts. I am
a conductor. I have gripped
live wires in my fist and felt currents
pulse in my fibres like blood.
I am steel, like the century.
I am the new epoch, rumbling like a tank
out of the future, towards you.

"Remember this: there is no law
but the law of steel, which is to say
all survivors learn to refine
the crude iron that blood contains
into armour, alloyed
with every element of cruelty
and tempered by beatings, injury and fear,
forged in the primal mould with crosses, bayonets
and machine-guns. There is no other law. These implements
have a half-life of centuries.

"I am Stalin

and my order is this: General 0——— will lead elements
of the Red Army stationed near Rostov south via Astrakhan
over the passes into Georgia. All resistance will be crushed
with indiscriminate fury. In Tiflis, Batum, Gori, anywhere
it appears. Crushed.

"People? Do my people still live there?
No. All dead. Take this down.

"I have no people. I am Stalin."

6. PHOTOGRAPH OF A GUTTED VILLAGE, GEORGIA

Should I be moved by this

Should I howl repentance and write poems
For the murdered comrade
And his wife, for the crippled child they would have beaten senseless
As soon as it could stumble

Should I dedicate psalms to the village mayor
Who slumped in the tavern every weeknight
Drunk, lecturing his witless electors,
Then tottering home to threaten his wife

Should I take up a collection
For the beggars who burned to death in the loft
Whose lives were a festering and a famishing
Who bred with the blind lust of dogs a line of stillborn sons

My comrade and his wife, the mayor, the village beggars,
Gone. This much, at least, I have corrected. You must understand
There are times these cratered vistas
Hold no nostalgia for me.
"Adorable Georgia"

Why should I be moved

Or weep and gather into my arms
The child squatting at the frame of the photograph, crooked
From beatings it took while still in the womb—

Perhaps it was the drunken mayor or his colleagues
Perhaps it was my murdered comrade
Whose brain at death hobbled back
Over its most brutal accomplishments, dreaming
Of blood as his eyes filled with it
Perhaps it was you my father, my father,
Why have you tormented me,
Twenty million times I have remembered

1922 (1949)

7. ELEGY IN EARLY WINTER

Nadezhda, it is snow they are calling for
from the Caspian Sea to Archangel.
And you are not here to see it.
With the rest of them you have disappeared
like the breath of old women at the doors
of cathedrals on Martyr's Day, like a widow's prayers
in winter, hoof prints on the tundra,
whatever will not be sustained through time
or language. Your flesh
has proven snow, and like the rest of them
you melt: white cells and singular crystals
trampled, muddied by the stiff boots
of soldiers in Red Square. The Army, the Kremlin,
exiles and internees, all insubstantial
as myrrh from a censer, yellowing leaves
in the annals of the dead. My own being
is all I can credit. I am real. I do not melt.
And these others—tonight, these cumulous others—
the wireless crying out for snow
from the Black Sea to Archangel.

1932

8. ON HITLER

The strong man sees his enemy not as an impediment but a catalyst. The enemy is a clandestine alloy without which metals can be made no stronger. Ultimately the difference between the strong and the weak inheres in this: that one man seeks and grapples with enemies, and evil, while the other avoids them for fear of vitiating the purity of his moral fibre. Which therefore rusts and crumbles away.

Evil is the philosopher's stone you must seek and seize and consume.

The weak are afraid of swallowing molten ore.

from a diary, Christmas 1943

9. TWO ELEGIES: A SON AND A COLLEAGUE

It will be said that now truly I have no people
because in Hitler I had found a kind of brother.
We held the same view of the dwarfs and freaks
who populate our earth with their squabbling litters,
for they are without ambition and therefore soulless.
     We have played for loftier stakes
and he has lost, though in his turn he made moves
that alarmed me, challenged me, made me stronger,
and took a son, my last true flesh, forever hostage.

from a letter, May 1945

10. TESTAMENT

Regret is for the foolish and temperamental. Cowards
call priests to their bedsides and repent.
The sentimentalist writes poems.
This is not a poem.
Knowing death is near, I set down this testament,
this explanation—no apology
and no poem.

1. The killings will emerge, no doubt of it. However ingeniously they are concealed, corpses will always find a way to surface. In a dream I saw thousands of them afloat on the Kura, pocked with sores and the bites of small fish, bloated with allegation. No doubt of it. I know power too well to pretend my memory, my statues, the cities named for me are safe from desecration.

2. An old priest from the provinces said to me once, On your deathbed you will remember God, and He you. The dying always reach out to Him: free-thinkers, libertines, ideological atheists, the most powerful politicians. Be careful He has not turned from you.

I wish the priest were here now so that I could spit in his beard and tell him I am not afraid. I did not leave the seminary because there is no God. I left the seminary to surpass God. I have surpassed God. I look forward to Our meeting should He exist, for I could crush Him also if I desired.

3. I remember a young poet. He talked of reading my verses in an old literary journal he discovered in some attic. He wept as he spoke to me, kissed my hand; he said I was a great poet and would I return to my writing. Into my palm he pressed a thin sheaf of papers.

I slapped him across the face and told him to move out of my way. Poetry is for dreamers, I told him. Look around you. Was this city, were these buildings, this nation, built on dreams? Do I look to you like a dream? What has the moon to do with Russia?

I crumpled his papers and threw them onto the pavement.

A nation is being built around you, bridges, airports, highways and factories, and you are writing poems. Do you think your pen, a million such as yours, could have stopped Hitler? When even the pen of a great poet like M——— proved useless against real power? I can't stand to think that young men believe such things. Leave me, I can't bear to look at you.

And of course he hurried away—lucky to be alive, he must have thought.

Regret is for fools, perhaps, but this I regret in weak moments.

I picked up the crumpled papers and took them with me. They were variations on my first poems, beautifully written, much better, I think, than the originals.

As I crossed names off my lists and signed warrants I found myself weeping, like a boy, weeping for the first time in years. I put the poems away in a drawer but the sentiment would not leave me. I had to burn every page before I could return to work.

11. "O POET, THE GEORGIANS HAVE PREPARED FOR YOU A MONUMENT IN HEAVEN"

At six I could swim in the River Kura. My friends shouted encouragement from the banks, though I knew they envied my strength and courage. The Kura's cold, glinting current attracted them but they were terrified of its darkness and depth. I was attracted but not afraid. I was at home in the current, glad for the impassable distance a few strokes could open between me and them. "Come back, Soso," they would begin to shout. "Come back to shore." And I would. On the banks we would wrestle until I threw them, one after another, into the mild shallows, where they thrashed and sputtered like apoplectics. Often I had to help them out.

Though I was the smallest of our group I was admired and feared and obeyed. Even then I sensed all around me an impotence, a cosmic docility that deferred to the rich, the strong, the determined. My family did not have money but I was strong for my age and determined.

At seven I caught smallpox. My face after the affliction was pocked and cratered as a battlefield, yet I found the disfigurement strangely appealing. As if I had been wounded gravely in some decisive conflict and was imperfectly healed; as if someone had pressed from my skin small tokens of an invaluable metal.

The poems came much later, though I was still a boy when I wrote them. They are perhaps a bit florid; I was filled at the time with a sentimental affection for Georgia and her past. I cherished the smells of the streets—from goat manure to *shashlik* and rosewater sweets—and the way Gori looked from the mountain under moonlight. I wanted to rip open my shirt and bare my breast to the moon. I wanted to stretch out my arms and worship the moon that showered the sleeping earth with light. *Know well*, I sang, *that those*

Who long ago succumbed to the oppressors
Will rise again and soar, winged with hope,
Above the sacred mountain . . .

At seventy it occurs to me (in facetious moments) that I have filled the sky thousands deep with soaring forms, there is hardly room for them to manoeuvre, they collide and plummet like massed cherubim in a religious tapestry. Though you would not want to call them oppressed; they were and are as vicious and debauched as the artists who prefigured them. I crushed them to the last man.

And don't bother pointing self-righteously at certain lines in my poetry; every author becomes a hypocrite with time. My actions have annulled all juvenile hypocrisy by overwhelming it with tides of actual blood. Ink is thin by contrast, the page pale.

A dictator is a poet of supreme accomplishments: his words are always heard and he can make them mean whatever he desires. He carves from the body of the world an order hewn in his own image. A god does no more.

1949

12. DEATHBED DREAM

but gori from the mountainhead was lovely in sunlight
an old man with a black walking stick
let me taste his tobacco he had fought at sebastopol
against the english and french the wars he sang me
were full of flags in blue wind and polished brass and white
horses how the river kura shimmered at noon I would swim there
and people on the banks were clapping
to see a child in the water they had meat and bread in woven hampers
winebottles glittered like ice and the hot sun
lit up a face among many it was nadezhda
years before I met her watching from the banks as I reached out
my hand I think she saw and toppled towards me into the river
disappearing quickly without a sign

CODA

Poet and dictator Josef Stalin was born in the town of Gori, Georgia, in December 1878.

His poems were written and published some twenty years before the Russian Revolution, when Georgia was a province of Czarist Russia. His name at the time was Josef Vissarionovich Djugashvili and he was a student in the Georgian Orthodox seminary in Tiflis. Years later, during his rise to power, he adopted the pseudonym "Stalin," a variant on the Russian word for steel.

He married Ekaterina Svanidze in 1904. Ten months later she died of complications associated with the birth of a son, Yakov. Soon after her death, Stalin left his ancestral province to pursue political ambitions in the north.

In 1921, two years after marrying his second wife, Nadezhda Alliluieva, he ordered the Red Army to return to Georgia and crush all counter-revolutionary resistance "with indiscriminate fury."

In 1932 Nadezhda Alliluieva died under mysterious circumstances. There is some reason to believe that Stalin might have murdered her after a quarrel. During the Second World War, Stalin's son from his first marriage, Yakov, was taken prisoner by the Nazis and later perished in one of Hitler's death camps.

The great Russian-Jewish poet Osip Mandelstam, first arrested in 1934 for writing a poem critical of Stalin's policy of collectivization, died in one of Stalin's own camps after his second arrest in 1938.

Stalin himself died in 1953.

MAN TO THE HILLS

RESTLESS

Man to the hills, woman to the shore
—Gaelic proverb quoted by Seamus Heaney in *Wintering Out*

Pensiones line Corfu Bay
but I followed the coast, then went inland.
The one form on a dry black road, I

cannot sleep on the banks of the sea.

And on Skye, when an overgrown cart-trail
ended in a cove by a ruined pier, I climbed
a gullswept cliff and slept in the hills, because I

cannot sleep on the banks of the sea.

Lay last on the brine-bitter
stones of Galway, my feet in flotsam
drying between tides, but woke soon
restless, thirsty and cold,
one form unlulled by the ocean, I

cannot sleep on the banks of the sea.

A PERISHABLE ART

I found my mother's footprints in the snow
still fresh, she'd passed this way only moments before.
Her tracks climbed and crossed the treeless hills at the skyline.
Her heels were halfmoon gouges in the white crust, glowing.

The prints held no warmth. Their shapes already changing.
Surprising how directly she had managed
to shear through that wandering terrain, as if
something unusual in the windempty range

of hills had captured her eye and drawn her on
with a purpose. And in fact all the signs there were
pointed to this—the long intervals between prints
suggesting haste, their unfaltering

evenness betraying a certain intensity, a certain
determination. I followed them some distance, saw nothing
but blue sky white hills and shadows between hills
and the prints themselves receding, as if by plan,

straight as a survey trail or concession road . . .
Before dark it grew windy. Powder snow
rippled like gauze curtains between hills, and quickly
filled in footprints—mine behind me
and my mother's before.

NATHAN

My brother lives
on the crippled rim.

He is this ward, this weary circumference
the city refuses. The city refuses him.

He is more thistle than poet's lilac.
He is the sun at evening
impaling itself on aerials.
He is a gasoline rainbow, he is a fragment
of slag, pierced
and worn as a black diamond.
He is none of these things.

Sometimes he leads me
into favourite streets, cracked and frost-heaved twenty winters,
though it's spring now, and evening, when
sun should be gold on the grass.
No grass on the crippled rim.
                                        At dusk
his city threadbare.
Country's tattered hem.
My brother lives here.

(From his mother's house you see the railway
lapsing into rushes; deserted fire-alleys full of sun.)
                                                            Tomorrow
has no future here
among cairns of refuse, the vagrant
tastes of auto buyers; I let Nathan veer
and speed behind a wreck's steering wheel.
From a yard there is talk, the brittle clink of glasses.

We take the street tonight, see houses
ramshackling white   yellow   black
in a row, like laid-off men
at a bar. In crooked doorways
women, bruised,
and children.
                                And in a yard of scrap steel Nathan toys
with clenched beer cans, clattering hubs
and tires, I lose him amid lines of drying washing,
there are blood smears on the city's hem, and
Nathan
Nathan, I call, as breezes belly a shirt
and reveal him staring up at something
torn, hung on the line
and waving—

some form still filling his father's shirt—

PHOTOGRAPHS OF MOUNTAINS

The face was the face of a stranger. It came upon him nearer now,
quite as one of those expanding fantastic images projected by the
magic lantern of childhood . . .
—Henry James, "The Jolly Corner"

His desk in those days faced a dark wall panelled
in counterfeit maple. Over the cracks, the imitation knots
and oddly symmetrical pattern he pasted photographs—
small spots of colour arranged
at eyelevel, like little panes of stained glass or even
mailslots on a dark door—open
to sudden light and a flurry of postcards
from remote places—

and the slot slapped closed.

So his mountains,
his sunblue portraits of slopes and long rows
of snowcliffs in the April light
(he tried to transpose them from frame
to the square page on his desk)
went dim,
himself, a small flaw
figured on a ridge
at the white margin
of a photograph, vanished
when he lowered the desklamp . . .

He left that room, the rooming house,
years ago and went west to settle
among mountains; wonders now if he returned
would he find those little windows
boarded up, drafts seeping through cracks in the panelling,
dust clotted in corners like the sediment of last year's snow—

and if on the way out the young climber he left
should pass him quite unexpectedly on the stairs—

DYLAN'S SOURCE

Green as a dungeon
he was chained
to the rain's ramshackling
spirits sailed
over hills of his saying

and tumbled
drunk as a gull
to the sea's sweet breadth—

At death
they carried him like a king
to a new dominion
his grinning lip
flecked amber
with a drop of drink
the shade and ringing
tone of rusted
chain

ABANDONED FIELDS

I sense the passing of woman   man
from black my earth
I feel the gap
of winter's opening
slowly into wasted fields,
these lapsing seasons leave us
grains of silt on snow—

There has been
a failure here: you sense the passion lost
in thinning woodsmoke, spiring
low through dwindling woodlots
in the jaws
the teeth
of east our wind—

I sense the going of woman   man
from rubbled farms
through churchyards rife
with unvoiced names
and past the meadow
where glaciers once
(in each our houses
rooms grow larger   halls
too long to walk   as words
are squandered in the open air   I
lose them seeping
cell by
cell
    by

phones we wait
in grey our woodrot houses
hours lean over cooling
woodstoves   mailslots
slacken
socket-empty—

A failure here
by stoves in-
tending fire
we leave
a snow of ash
no flame
                    I sense
time's passion
cold
as cordwood   fields
abandoned)

NEAR PULPIT ROCK

I've lied about mountains—
carved them into metaphors, symmetrical
as the slave-raised peaks
at Giza.
I've called them gods, explained them
with elaborate myths, made them
spires of men's desiring . . .

I walked—I thought I walked—
through templed elm and aisles
of pine trees, steepled
from the seacoast
to this choral shore,
I walked

and always lied.
But no lies of mine
could make the mountains
new. I saw at second-last these peaks
are not even indifferent.

Saw last the Funeral Range
where shapes a thousand men tall
lie—I'd say scarred and sacred,
even name them pyramids, but

understand what that would mean
in the absence
of any buried king.

Nahanni River, 1985

INUKSHUK

We found him first in early spring

standing alone under the eye-
teeth of an inland range

a stunted form, bewildered
by the longer shadows of peaks
he cast
an image, dim
as a minute hand

and circled hours on snow.

We passed him again in August
on a wide plain rimmed
with brilliant hills

worn smaller now, the body
rimed with lichen, limbs
blunt gestures of shale—

quarried once in the low hills
he had been changed
the tundra conspiring around him

to this
dune of rubble
like sand in an hourglass

we tracked his gaze to the lowland.

And September, with the new hail
cobbling the seacoast
we found him at last, eroded
grey as beached bone

a dwarf
aging among barrows he
saw us push from shore
leaving as his makers had—

his face could not even accuse
but bore betrayal
with the amazed endurance
of a likeness, unfinished,
or a forgotten god.

(Inukshuk *are man-like stone cairns erected by the ancestors of modern Inuit to divert migrating caribou and mark the routes to the sea. The word means "like a man."*)

THE SCREAM [1893]

Supposing he inhabits a kind of hell, the figure freezes
near the canvas margin, on a high bridge
traversing some northern scene. It's the turn of the season—

things suggest this, the light, invidious and thin,
dazing, desolate slope of ridge
and bald hills and the aspect of chapel

with its scattered houses. The figure itself is pale or, better, un-
faced and drained by a wind we might suppose
comes from our direction: a place of estranged viewers, living

in a future that sends autumn and this blood-pall
dusk. It's the era-to-come, unsettling the seaboard
with gusts that screech and warn in the rigging

of a minute ship bound—where? Nothing provides
an answer. Outward, we assume, from the narrowing fjord
into open sea, though it seems detained

by a vague inertia, caught up in invisible tides
and stalled in the frame where walkers, unsolicitous, pass,
and the figure, like an afterthought or image retained

on the retina, presses to its ears
hard questions: and screams
headlong into wind so we cannot hear.

THE MACHINE GUNNER

I saw them. They came like ghosts out of ground-
mist, moving
over ruined earth in waves, running,

no, walking, shoulder to shoulder
like a belt of bullets or like
men: tinned meat lined on a conveyor belt as the sun

exploded in thin shafts on metal
buckles, bayonets, the nodding
spires of helmets. I heard faint battle cries

and whistles, piercing through the shriek
of fire and iron falling, the slurred
cadence of big guns. As they funnelled

like a file of mourners into gaps
in the barbed wire I made quick
calculations and slipped the safety catch.

But held my fire. Alongside me
the boys in the trenches worried them with
rifles, pistols, hand grenades,

but they came on, larger now, their faces
almost resolving out of hazed, hot
distance, their ranks at close quarters amazing

with dumb courage, numb step, a sound of drugged
choking in gas and green mud, steaming . . .
Who were these men. I saw them penitent,

sagging to knees. I saw their dishevelled
dying. And when finally they broke
into a run it came to me

what they had always been, how I'd always,
really, seen them: boys
rushing toward us with arms

outstretched, hands clenched as if in urgent prayer,
sudden welcome or a reunion
quite unexpected. Yes. And more than this

like children, chased by something behind the lines
and hurrying to us
for rescue—

I spat and swung the gun around. Fired,
felt the metal pulse
and laid them three deep in the wire.

THE ANGEL

In the cockpit, under the glass pod,
the sibilance of oxygen becomes
a figure breathing
in intervals behind my seat: breathing
into tubes and mask,
co-pilot, we are flying into perilous airspace.

In the cockpit, death
inhabits every sound: switches click
and rattle by my chest, the radio's
râle of static expires,
to either side the engines scream, ecstatic.
                                                            Ascent
is a function of dials
and fine control, in minutes earth is blurred under iron
wings, I sense blossoming
cloud, the contours of diminishing
coastlines (my flesh is a fraction
in this design,
                        nothing more.
I did not build this structure. I am sent
instructions in a babble of code and static:
sounds of leaves brittle underfoot, a map
crumpling into flame).
                                    I repeat,
this was not my design.
I am neither fuel nor engine, no
line in death's agenda: I am
spirit: my breath moves
beyond the blue-
print, my touch is warm. The sum

of my heart is more
than an order:

Over a target
you will focus

the cross-hair scope
your crucifix

you are word of steel, they
the flesh made number

now

DECIPHERING THE PASSAGE

In blade-silver straits between islands even summer
was stillborn, endangered as the adamant songs
of gulls deserting into fogs above the passage

they did not discover. Twin ships lashed by anchor cords
indivisibly to their extinction. Well-crafted hulls
crushed by shards of puzzling ice, sharp white as the un-

marked fringes of maps, or English timbers
beached and bleaching under the blind-
folded hills. A certain shade of white, but not

the white of certainty, that fabric of a virginal century's
premise, torn. White of the whale, winter's bones
scrimshawed with piercing weather. *The Erebus. The Terror*,

the terror. To see that tone stare at the page's edge until snow-
blind as the sailors at their dying, staggering
south into gales, white of blizzard, hail, cracked shore-stones and

this
untouched sheet
of ice, as I fill its pale
                                        (white
whalers peering from the foredeck
of search boats into the freezing)
                                                            surface
with terms of unlikely rescue . . .

                                                            Sir John sailed with a cargo

of proofs, many charts
mapping the misty transition
from history to incoherence;
                                        on his maps
a white fiercer than unblotted parchment,
a mutinous, consuming
pallor hinted

there is no passage here for men
from Devon and Somerset
who have sturdy sons and delicate
faithful wives
Whose whole world will become a margin
clenched white around their ships—

                                    John Franklin did not discover his aim
but a whiteness in every sound as patient
and impartial as icebergs
awaiting the blind
century sailing onward, credulous, captained by a sane
faith in progress
that read meaning into every passage
because it was sailing ahead too fast, an evolutionary
defect

        debris
grinding the littoral under heads
where gravestones of three men face north like sentries
across a frozen sound
with no one left to inform
of anything

a hundred more who scrawled
a linear history
in snow and cairns stuffed with rope and empty tins and polished
bones a cold spring south to Victory
Point
then perished
in duned waves
Brittania never ruled—
refuted
by blinding storms
the hoar
face of a spreading earth
hauling behind them a life
boat full of England

able in the end
to lift around them with only voices
a fleeting shanty
of song

ENGLISH CEMETERY, GASPÉSIE

In a corner of the yard, quiet
And discreetly removed from worn, grey-
Shouldered monuments, you find the least
Ancient headstones weathering uneasily
On the lip of a seacliff. Giving onto the gulf
And east winds, these smaller markers glow
White as sails in the sun's offing; lean in the gust
Like fishermen over a deck's edge. On the brink
Of a shrinking headland, stripped willows
Hunch and quaver.
                    Even the clearest of the stones
Seem to list into whispering
sallow earth, *Sacred*
To the Heart of Susannah Jane Tom Sommers
is laid here, and John Francis Mahon, who
Died on the Magdalen River 1910 and left
no one behind
                (except
perhaps the inscriber—)

Other stones are not so easy to read.
Only seventy years have sanded them,
salted them white until
now in the annulling sunlight
they are wholly illegible—runes
in an abandoned tongue,
ideas on a blank slate—

but someone must have carved them
once, cracked them in stone
with strong hands and Anglican assurance believing
they would endure for centuries

The yard however is empty at my visit—
no English speakers live
so far east now
their last words engraved years ago

And lying among them somewhere
the scribe, a nameless sexton
who did double-duty with chisel and spade
the last of his enclave
to die perhaps
wondering in the end
who would keep the lawn trimmed
who polish and clean the stones

aware at his last sigh
of a mute wind
hammering the walls

GLOUCESTER AND THE SIRENS

Tensed on the cliff's extreme verge
I feel the winds urging me
look
        below in the spiralling valley
the tarn a rich, vertiginous green
compelling me with silence
compelling me

and I have gone as far as this: to listen
to the wind in void spaces, keening
at my shoulders, whirling
in the vortices . . .

These are the voices we do not own
that speak to us in unguarded places
of the deaths of selves, impending lives
—the innuendo of a ventriloquist
at large in the body's darkness—

"As I dreamed, voices rose like echoes from the gorge,
I was hearing myself speak and I was afraid—"

We saw you on the precipice like a blind man
needing help to die,
then we saw behind you with hands readied
—you again. We were afraid to call out to one
because of the other. So we said nothing.

“—from the gorge words rose from the gorge
in infinite recession, dreams within dreams, and I heard *We sleep*
between two open jaws,
a closing darkness, there is a life
we want to push into existence—”

And you will go as far as this: grant the winds
a cold hearing, learn the logic of their seductions,
even let yourself dream
of plummeting through these idle spaces
where syllables hang in the air undone

Maligne Amphitheatre

EPITAPH: FOR THE RUINED LIBRARY, DRESDEN

HERE LIES

(stacked in catacombs of slowly
decomposing paper and ash, dust
jackets breathe
the studious aroma
of silted silence, deathsmell
of scorched parchment
scrolled
in passages like children

crouching in the underground)

LIE

Where scholars stalked, a winter
under ruins
has canticled halls
with hymns of ice
suspended, they
drip notes between stone
shelves, descending strata
of theorum and map,
thin scraps
of pamphlets, tomes entombed,
the drafts
of unperfected poems—

Elsewhere among blackened carrels lie
volumes of antique argument,
abandoned adagios, proofs
and reproofs, Plato
and Pascal's wager

cast now by insects,
the scrawling maggot, reductive worms,
who bore like scholars through stacks
and aisles of amazed soil—
the whiterobed stoics
whom no one could refute—
I commend these lines
to the perennial librarian.

THE BURNED-OUT SLOPE

Skull-shapes in deadfall, sockets in rotting pine
reprove our slow approach
with anthropomorphic eyes.

Where whitened horns record the sun's transits
charred trunks tapered by years
fill an east wind with invisible spores,
feeding saxifrage and lichen,
fuelling cycles of unchanging flux . . .

And I am here
after trying so long to exile
the imperious eye
to listen with ear primed
at the rock's heart
for the swarming of molecules
the sullen locutions of an empty land
—lake wind river stone
fire that clambered up these slopes
like cloudshadow over a mountainside
with or without us making forests fall
and carving symbols of them.

Elk Lake

POEM

In this hired room, my window
gives onto torn sea, insinuates

slats between stanzas of foam,
long lines of breakers, scrolling

slowly into noise. I can hear them
stamp, erase this littoral, even the break-

water barely holds them—(in my dream
I drift outward like a liminal thing

against a wind that is deafening
shore and land; it's a poem I have been

nearing from the first, by instalment
like the tides, at a leased window, giving

onto perpetuity. And in time, these slats
are going to rust and freeze. Like lips, sealed

after the words are done. Like a fastened diary.
Crack

through the spaces lean out and scream———)

Chandydassa, Bali

NIGHTMARE

I will be standing
on the verge of a plain
by a highway no one else has taken

Flat dance of the skyline
skin seared by a treeless sun
somewhere the roar of an ocean

                                        or a silver car
that slows   stops
a door that swings

and I must choose
on the verge of the plain—
and though it is hard to see

through the layering dust
I believe I hoist my bag and
pull it after me

into that car,

INQUEST

Why am I drawn often by the icy
interstices between stars
or arctic islets, the notion
of radio waves nobody received
disbanding over atmosphere

There is some need some nostalgia
that makes me savour
high plains when they are most empty
the intimations of human dailyness
any ruin leaves behind

For some time, my heart
has been a long distance runner
of steppes the sun cindered or snow interred,
that were mind-mapped by vanished peoples,
though more than their names drew me:
                                        Great Bear Lake,
the Belly River, Black Rapids,
Dark Harbour and the Hungry Hills,
                                        I have been consumed
by the actual wreckage of age,
the brittle dignity of pyramids,
of light in columns falling
through Doric ruins, a ring
of Dorset houses holy to me
in its cold corrosion

Why in my most contemporary summer
were crowded beaches always blind
under Meursault's sun, and yet

beautiful—did the empty quarters that drew me
mirror some quadrant in the heart—
no inquest can ever show—

(See the young man in the mirror,
staring, self-concerned as a tightly
closed poem, soon the entropy
that pulls stars apart
will fold him into himself
like foothills, rift valleys,
glacial drift, dry riverbeds
grown over when the climate changed—

Moved with words or by them
was he carried ahead of his body
into silence—

Wind over the tundra tells you nothing)

THE GAP

Thought you'd left, then
sensed your steps
nearing through the bark black room, you
nudged the wind chimes
    (icicles on swaying boughs
        bracelets brushed undressing)

                                                            pendent
face above me
near as my own
winter breath, yet sky-
remote as cirrus—

loved and let the arching instant
drain all distance
                                anger
                                        all—

so breathe deep
colour by my neck
feel it flickering there
A dripping bough or dreaming
fingers leafing through my hair

COBALT PEAK

On the shrugged shoulder
of Cobalt Peak
a bubbling drumlin amplifies
the lowland language
hushed and strange
marred by echoes
far as cars
that slip down
hissing
highway
veins

Her veins beat sky-blue,
hot below, above the tattered
hands of cloud, outside the tent
that severs sightlines,
                                        letting sounds
sing through unchanged—

You let the col
the col call back
your words
your words
your veins   to peak
the pounding drumlin amplifies
my love your cries
my love your cries

INVENTION

Tell me the word, mother, if you know now,
The word known to all men.

Because she had watched seedlings grow
too often through double-panes of her storm
window;

because pineneedles, honed by sunlight,
brushed the screen softly but
would not penetrate its mesh

she invented a garden
indoors, under a bay window,
filling it with herbs.

                    Still, it was the word
for each plant she thought of first
on waking: tarragon,
ivy and lavender, sorrel, coriander,
rue. The double names recited themselves
in her halfsleep: nightshade,
rattlegrass and goldenrod,
heart's ease.
            And when she walked up the sunpaved hall
to her garden,
the lambent blossoms,
the slight wavering stalks that might have belonged
in a bird's delicate skeleton

filled the room with a forest
of syllables, green
and speechless as a bird's call—

tangible as first metaphor:

Eden.

LOVERS

1

Lovers are stone-
deaf and soft limbs, drawing
flesh in earth
tones together, colour to skin
and gently
breath

in sheets they are sculpting
slopes, rift valleys, sown
with dry flints,
blood and boneshards . . .

20,000 years ago on the glazed
wet walls of a cave
in Central Europe an artist
shaped with hollow bones and blown ochre
two lovers
small and tangled they appear to be
shrubs or some other disturbance on a long horizon
until you look closely, love,
here

and here, on this brittle scroll
of Chinese rice paper, see two
lovers limned in watercolour
in a landscape of pillowy cliffs,
waterfalls & soft waterbirds
feathered on vaporous sky. Each
time we love this way in our land-
scape we play again that fragile
score you almost hear, that same
delicate, distant mouth music . . .

2

Cobalt Peak, Alberta

Your belly was likened once
to fields of wavering grain
but here by the col where no
grain waves, I
dream of hotter regions, drier,
the pulsing undulations of open plain, savannah
hemmed by remote hills
where vague shapes trample their dusty shadows
and I am running, a slowing
form at the dawn,
toward whatever form it is
couples with the skyline.
On the plain behind me, tors
are receding peak
by peak
like the wrecked portals
of exhausted city-states,

200,000
years ago or longer—

behind me epochs slam closed like a row of doors.

3

and you are stone-
deaf and soft limbs
for the instant outside of history
you arch beside me
above me
or under

you let the col
the col call back
your words
your words
your veins, to peak

in China and the plains of Africa
Europe and the Coastal Range
these lovers are the soil we walk on

SKY BURIAL

The primary form of funeral in Tibet involves hacking a dead person's body into small segments, which are left to the mountain birds. In a few hours only the bones remain; they are ground with the barley meal tsampa *that was the person's staple in life and now constitutes the soil to which he or she is returned.*

Hide of stone slabs, slopes in mist
swooping down to temple yards,
to a thousand small cairns like the graves of eagles—

by the mountain, birds soar in hungry loops,
mandalas in thin air, prayer kites
whirling before the plunge—

          Each day somebody dies in Lhasa,
by dawn they are out to render him air,
give her to sky and birds that are the sky's hunger
          so as the thud of an axe dies off
and birds coil downward in their patient spools
you seem to see a human form feathered on air, a figure
          free at last to straddle
updrafts off the mountainhead, slough hides of stone, grey
slabs, slip free
          of skin, as a monk at his dying might
walk away from monastery walls
that were never more than a method and a framing
          into ascetic hills above the high plain, over
cairns and scriptured cliffs
          to throw off like stained paper his maroon
robes:
          receive the wind

Lhasa, October 1986

ACKNOWLEDGMENTS

Poems from *Stalin's Carnival* appeared first—and, in the case of several anthologized poems, subsequently—in the following magazines and anthologies. The author remains very grateful to the editors of all these publications: *Agni, Anthos, Antigonish Review, Arc, Ariel, Dalhousie Review, Event, Exile, The Fiddlehead, 15 Canadian Poets X 3* (Oxford University Press, 2013, Gary Geddes, ed.), *Grain, Grind, Lines Review, The Literary Review, Matrix, Modern Canadian Poets* (Carcanet, 2010, Evan Jones & Todd Swift, eds), *Moosehead Review, The New Canon* (Signal Editions, 2005, Carmine Starnino, ed.), *The New Quarterly, Next Exit, Poetry Australia, Poetry Canada Review, Poets '88* (Quarry Press, 1988, Bob Hilderley & Ken Norris, eds), *Prism International, Prospice, Quarry, Queen's Quarterly, Québec Suite* (The Muses' Company, 1995, Endré Farkas, ed.), *Revue Europe* (French translations by Judith Cowan), *Taproot, Thru The Smoky End Boards* (Polestar, 1996, Kevin Brooks & Sean Brooks, eds), *University of Windsor Review, Wascana Review*, and *Waves*.

Author photo by Monique de St. Croix